If our love were a book ...

...this is how
it would look.

IF OUR LOVE WERE A BOOK… THIS IS HOW IT WOULD LOOK

Summersdale Publishers Ltd
46 West Street
Chichester
West Sussex
PO19 1RP
UK

www.summersdale.com

Printed and bound in China

ISBN: 978-1-84953-337-9

Substantial discounts on bulk quantities of Summersdale books are available to corporations, professional associations and other organisations. For details contact Summersdale Publishers by telephone: +44 (0) 1243 771107, fax: +44 (0) 1243 786300 or email: nicky@summersdale.com.

TO Will

FROM Natalie

If I were a palm
In a faraway land,
You could rest in my shade
And snooze in the sand.

If I were Romeo
And I'd not met you yet,
When our paths crossed at last
I'd ditch old Juliet.

If I were a **boat**
I'd keep you afloat.

If I were a **map**
And you had lost your way,
I would **help** you find the path
To send you on your way.

If I were a pair of shoes
I'd take you round the town,
Looking like a superstar
And never falling down.

If I were a **bed**...
Enough said!

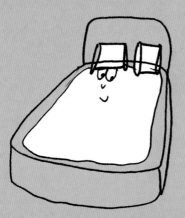

If I were a **unicorn**
That only you could see,
It would mean a lot to know
That you **believed in me.**

If I were a **dream**
And I were yours to keep,
I'd make your dreams come **true by day,**
Not only in your sleep.

If I were a grazed **knee**
Or some other injury,
I know you'd be caring
And take good care of me.

If I were **paper**
And you picked me from the pile,
I'd become for you a folded swan
Just to see you **smile**.

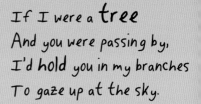

If I were a **tree**
And you were passing by,
I'd **hold** you in my branches
To gaze up at the sky.

If I were a swing
I'd make your heart sing.

If I were made of **glue**
I'd **stick** myself to you.

If I were a **tickle**
I'd wriggle on your skin,
You'd try to stop your giggles
Till you couldn't keep them in.

If I were a **ghetto blaster**
And you loved the crazy beat,
I'd play some music just to see you
Dancing down the street.

If I were a glass of wine
Or two or three or four,
You would keep me company
Until we hit the floor.

If I were a hat
Of incredible style,
I'd be honoured just to sit
On your head for a while.

If I were a **hug**
I'd wrap you up tight,
So when you were sad
You'd soon feel alright.

If I were a **fairy**
I would grant all your wishes,
Jewels, fine wine, designer shoes...
...and washed-up dirty dishes!

If I were a chocolate cake
sitting on the shelf,
I'd invite you to a feast
And sacrifice myself.

If I were John Lennon
And my feelings for you grew,
I'd have left The Beatles
To spend all my time with you.

If I were your **beard**
I hope you'd never shave,
Even if I itched a bit
And made you look like **Dave**.

If I were Little Jack Horner
I'd want you in my corner.

If I were a DVD
I'd just show films of
you and me.

If I were an echo
And you began to shout,
I wouldn't mind a little noise
To get your feelings out.

If I were a **London bus**
And you were running late,
You could wave for me to stop —
I'd never make you wait.

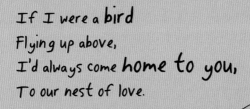

If I were a **bird**
Flying up above,
I'd always come **home to you,**
To our nest of love.

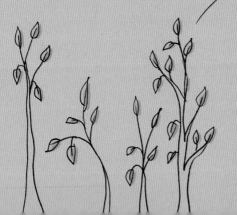

If I were Little Bo Peep
I'd ask you to help find my sheep.

If I were an alien
Flying in from Mars,
I'd come to Earth and beam you up
And show you wondrous stars.

If I were **Bonnie**
And met you before Clyde,
I'd walk a **straight** and narrow path
With you there by my side.

If I were your kitten
I'd be smitten.

If I were your **hair**
People would stop and stare.

If I were Humpty Dumpty
And you walked by my wall,
I know that you would help me
If I, perchance, should fall.

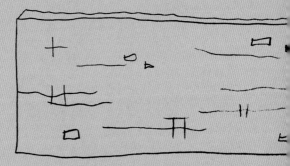

If I were a bit of fluff
In your best coat's pocket,
I'd make that coat my happy home
And hope you'd NEVER wash it.

If I were a silly voice
And found you late at night,
We could stay up laughing
Until the morning light.

If I were a big **balloon**
With nothing much to do,
We could fly for months and months
Just looking at the view.

If I were a pair of **socks**
The ones you're given yearly,
I'd be prepared to touch your feet,
Just kidding... no not really!

If I were a **laptop**
Whose lap would I choose?
The **loveliest** lap of all is **yours**
So how could I refuse?

If I were Bob Dylan
And you were my muse,
I'd write a classic love song
So your heart I'd never lose.

If I were a **duster**
I'd make the world dust-free,
Cleaning every corner
While you **drank your cup of tea.**

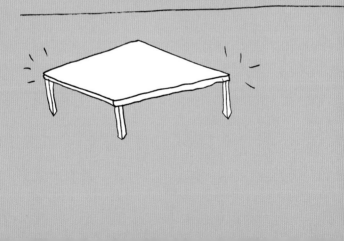

If I were a lawn
Waiting for a mow,
You could lie upon my grass
And watch the flowers grow.

If I were an onion
And I was cut in two,
I'd be so sad to make you cry
That I would cry with you.

If I were ants
I'd like to live in your pants.

If I were Mona Lisa
Enigmatic and beguiling,
For others I would simply gaze
But for you I would be smiling.

If I were an **angel**
Then that would make us **two**,
I'm in heaven as I've found
Someone as nice as you.

If you're interested in finding out more about our
gift books, follow us on Twitter: @Summersdale

SUMMERSDALE.COM
LASTLEMON.COM